THE SHANG DYNASTY OF ANCIENT CHINA

THE HISTORY DETECTIVE INVESTIGATES

Geoff Barker

WAYLAND

First published in 2014 by Wayland

Copyright © Wayland 2014

Wayland
338 Euston Road
London NW1 3BH

Wayland Australia
Level 17/207 Kent Street
Sydney, NSW 2000

The History Detective Investigates series:

Produced for Wayland by
White-Thomson Publishing Ltd
www.wtpub.co.uk
+44 (0)843 208 7460

Editor: Geoff Barker
Designers: Alix Wood and Ian Winton
Consultant: Philip Parker
Proofreader: Lucy Ross

A catalogue record for this title is available from the British Library.

ISBN: 978-0-7502-8174-4

Dewey Number: 931'.02-dc23

Printed in Malaysia

Wayland is a division of Hachette Children's Books, an Hachette UK company

Picture Acknowledgments: Stefan Chabluk: 5t; **Dreamstime:** 14 (Anekoho), 15t (Christineg), 29t (Jun Mu); **Getty Images:** 18 (O. Louis Mazzatenta); **Shutterstock:** cover t and 19b (cnyy), 2 and 15b (Jun Mu), 5b (Meiqianbao), 10 (Grigvovan), 11t (chinahbzyg), 11b (tenten10), 17c (Ekaterina Garyuk), 17b (sunxuejun), 19t (PhotoStock10), 29b (Fedor Selivanov); **SuperStock:** 8 (DeAgostini), 9 (TAO Images), 24t (DeAgostini), 24b (Fotosearch); **Gary L.Todd:** 7, 20, 22; **TopFoto:** 4 (The Granger Collection); **Wikimedia Commons:** cover b, folios and 26 (Editor at large), 1 and 21t (Rosemania), 6 (Ma Lin), 12 (www.GaryLeeTodd.com), 13 (Saad Akhtar), 16 (BabelStone), 21b (Shizhao), 23t (PericlesofAthens), 23b (Mlogic), 25, 27t and 27b (Mountain), 28 (Vassil); **Alix Wood:** 17t.

Above: This turtle shell has writing from the Shang dynasty.

Previous page: Yin was an ancient Shang city. Historians discovered many treasures there during the last century.

Cover (top): The Yellow River.

Cover (bottom): Shang bronze axe-head.

CONTENTS

Words in **bold** can be found in the glossary on page 30.

The history detective Sherlock Bones will help you to find clues and collect evidence about the Shang dynasty. Wherever you see one of Sherlock's paw-prints, you will find a mystery to solve. The answers are on page 31.

WHO WERE THE SHANG?

The Shang dynasty, or ruling family, controlled an area in the North China Plain in ancient China from around 1600 BCE to 1046 BCE. The Shang's territory extended from beyond the Yellow River as far as the East China Sea and into the Yangzi River valley to the south. Compared to the size of China today, the land governed by the Shang dynasty may not seem very large. However, the Shang way of life and its culture spread far beyond its own borders.

DETECTIVE WORK

Find out more about the Shang. Some historians divide the Shang era into three separate periods. Carry out a search at www.britishmuseum.org to discover what the three different periods are called. Start by typing 'shang dynasty' in the search box.

Before the Shang came to power, the Xia dynasty may have ruled this part of China from around 2070 BCE to 1600 BCE. This version of history is based mainly on Chinese texts from over 2,000 years ago. The lack of further evidence makes it hard to say whether the Xia definitely existed or not. There may well have been a dynasty before the Shang, but little is known about this period.

This human figure is made of jade, a hard stone that is difficult to carve. Its design shows the skill of the Shang artist.

Chinese dynasties could succeed or fail, depending on who was in charge. Frances Wood, curator of the Chinese collection at the British Library, explained how ancient Chinese historian Sima Qian (c.145 BCE-86 BCE) *'introduced the idea… that dynasties begin with the very virtuous and noble founder, and then they continue through a series of rulers until they come to a bad last ruler, and he is so morally* **depraved** *that he is overthrown.'*

The Shang sites of Yin and Huanbei are near modern-day Anyang, while the city of Shang is found close to today's Zhengzhou.

🐾 **Look at the map. What do the Chinese words Huang He mean?**

Shang people lived in a number of smaller settlements in northern China before creating their first walled city, near the Yellow River. Secure here, the Shang fought frequent battles against small neighbouring **clans** and larger states. The Shang people lived in at least five different capitals, one after the other. These include Shang, the early city near modern-day Zhengzhou, and the last Shang capital, Yin (at today's Anyang).

The Shang dynasty created a central government that was very well organized. At the head of this was a powerful king. He was supported by noblemen, and many of them were part of his own family. Shang kings were **ambitious** and had many big projects. They gathered together vast numbers of Shang people to work toward common goals. The most important of these were fighting battles, labouring on the land and helping to build new cities. The Shang increased the number of their workers by capturing soldiers from nearby clans and turning them into prisoners to work for them.

The Shang dynasty made great cultural advances during the Chinese **Bronze Age**. By the late Shang period, from around the thirteenth century BCE, skilled craftspeople were producing beautiful bronze works of art.

This intricate wine container, shaped like a dragon, is called a 'gong'.

WHAT DID SHANG KINGS DO?

The first Shang king is known as Tang, or Tai Yi. He defeated Jie, believed by many to be the last ruler of the previous dynasty, the Xia. In all, thirty different Shang kings stayed in power for well over five centuries, until around 1046 BCE.

King Tang is thought to have established the dynasty's first capital at Shang, near modern-day Zhengzhou.

The king's most important role was to act as chief priest. He was the only person who could contact his dead **ancestors**. The royal ancestors could in turn communicate with the supreme god Shang Di. This special relationship with the dead meant that the king was believed to be the closest living being to a god. The king had a busy time consulting his ancestors and had to make important decisions for himself, his family and his kingdom.

Shang kings carried out several other vital roles, ruling this part of ancient China with great efficiency. Living in the capital, the king counted on the support of noblemen from his own city, as well as noble warriors from nearby settlements.

DETECTIVE WORK

See if you can find out the names of some of the Shang kings. Find out more about the way the kings governed their kingdom. See www.education.com/ Do a search for 'shang dynasty'. Look under the heading of 'Government' for more information.

Shang kings put great numbers of men to work on the land. It was the king who announced when crops had to be planted in the fields. He may also have been the one to decide if the kingdom needed to change its capital, which happened many times during the Shang era. No-one knows exactly why the Shang moved so often. Perhaps disease or natural disasters, such as flooding, caused them to choose a new capital. The king probably consulted his ancestors. If the ancestors told him it was no longer safe to stay in the capital, everyone had to move. This meant building a whole new city. Shang kings used thousands of men to construct these new settlements.

Kingship passed from the elder brother to his younger brothers. Sisters in the same family were not allowed to become queen. If there were no brothers left, kingship then passed from uncle to nephew.

The last king, Di Xin, is often portrayed as physically strong. He is also seen as an unfair, **dissolute** leader. Under his poor rule, the Shang grew weaker, while the neighbouring Zhou state began to gain in power. The Zhou eventually allied with nearby peoples and overthrew the Shang.

What animals were used to pull the king's chariot?

King Di Xin was the last king of the Shang dynasty. China's first great historian, Sima Qian, wrote about the king's strengths and weaknesses:

'[Di Xin's] **disposition** was sharp, his **discernment** was keen, and his physical strength excelled that of other people. He fought ferocious animals with his bare hands. He considered everyone [to be] beneath him. He was fond of wine… and doted on women…'

Shang kings used a horse-drawn chariot on hunts and during battles.

HOW DID THE SHANG WAGE WARS?

The kings of the Shang dynasty waged many wars against nearby states. The kings often assembled between 3,000 and 5,000 troops to fight their opponents. These numbers rose to as many as 13,000 soldiers during the biggest battles. Shang kings built their dynasty on the superiority of their mighty armies. As a result, this successful ruling family stayed in power in this region of ancient China for over five hundred years.

With the help of noblemen, the king was able to plan and fight wars against neighbouring enemies. Noblemen from the capital city and nearby friendly settlements provided the king with vast numbers of peasants as **infantry** (foot soldiers). As well as having large numbers of infantry, the Shang gained a further advantage over their enemies in battle by using bronze weapons. They made sturdy metal weapons including bronze-tipped spears with heavy axe heads. Shang soldiers were also able to defend themselves with shields.

The Shang king often had to decide how many soldiers he needed to fight against an enemy. This historical account records preparation for battle:

'This season the king raises 5,000 men to campaign against the Tufang.'

What metal was the dagger-axe head made from?

Mounted on a long wooden handle, the ornate bronze dagger-axe was a lethal weapon.

The main reason for the Shang soldiers' superiority, however, was their use of chariots. The Shang's enemies did not have any chariots, but the Shang king and many of his nobles went into battle on horse-drawn chariots which were large enough to carry three people. One drove the chariot, while the noble warrior, from a high, standing position, had room to swing his long-handled dagger-axe. The archer was also free to fire his bow from the platform. The Shang bow was made of wood, bone and horn: it was very strong, with a long range. Chariots were quicker and more mobile than foot soldiers who could easily get bogged down in exhausting, hand-to-hand combat.

After the battles, Shang soldiers seized the enemy's food, precious metals and **livestock**. They also took as many prisoners as they could. These captives helped the Shang kings when they needed huge numbers of men to build their fortified cities. Prisoners suffered terribly under this backbreaking physical labour. These captives were often killed as **sacrifices** to the Shang gods.

DETECTIVE WORK

The wheel is one of the world's greatest inventions. Find out when and where wheels were first used. What did early versions look like? Find out more at http://library.thinkquest.org/C004203/science/science02.htm

Two horses pulled the chariot at the front, while three soldiers stood on the platform at the back.

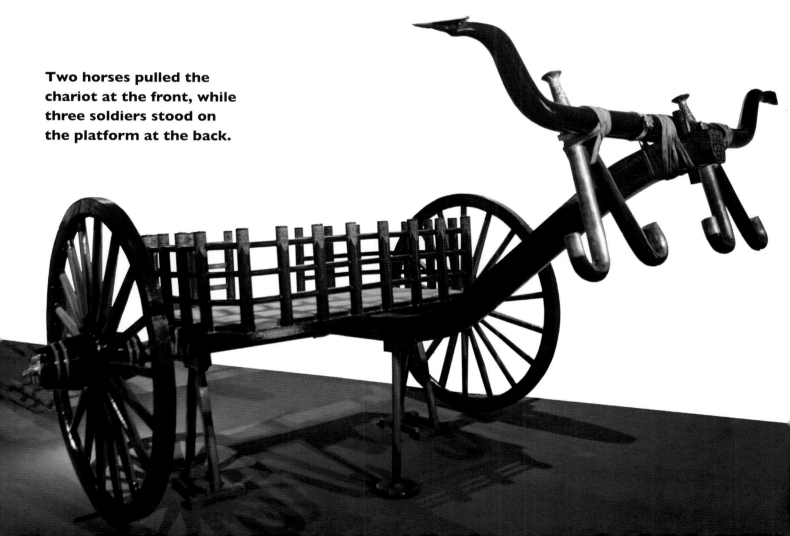

WHAT DID ORDINARY PEOPLE DO?

Most Shang people were peasants who worked hard in the fields. More than three thousand years ago, the valley region around the Yellow River had a climate that was both wetter and warmer than today. The land was very fertile and suitable for growing crops such as millet, as well as some rice and wheat. The peasants used simple wooden or stone tools to cultivate the land.

Peasants were forced to work in the fields to make sure the kings and nobles had plenty of food. The Shang kings and nobles **exploited** the masses so life was very harsh for ordinary people. When peasants finished working long days in the fields, they returned to their homes outside the city walls. They lived in pits dug into the ground, which were covered by material to make a very simple roof. The Shang raised cattle, sheep and chickens, but peasants ate whatever food was available, most likely grains and vegetables. Skeletons uncovered in **excavations** and examined by scientists show that peasants were badly nourished during the Shang era.

DETECTIVE WORK

Find out more about the different social classes in Shang civilization. Look at the 'social classes' section in this short video on the Shang dynasty at www.youtube.com/watch?v=Q8ZjHayRzQs

In some places in China today, work in the fields is not so different from Shang times.

Peasants wore very basic clothing. Typically, this was a long jacket, tied at the waist, and trousers woven out of plant material such as hemp. Winters were harsh and these clothes would have been uncomfortable during wet and cold conditions in the open fields. There were no schools during the Shang period, so peasants did not receive any education. Only the nobles were encouraged to read and write.

As well as farming the land for the kings and nobles, peasants also had to perform other duties. They had to fight battles for them, and help to build walled cities. They also had to dig deep royal tombs when their kings died. As an artisan, life was much easier. Shang artisans were the skilled craftspeople who made bronze **vessels**, such as wine goblets and large bowls. These were valuable pieces made especially for Shang ceremonies and **rituals**. A few of these highly skilled artisans were lucky enough to live within the walls of the capital city.

During the Shang era, the grain millet was the main crop.

Small and light, cowry shells were used to buy goods.

Gathered from the South China Sea, cowry shells were the main form of currency in Shang times. This **inscription** shows their value:

'Upon his return the king rewarded him with… the cowries which were captured in the expeditions against Yung'.

🐾 **How did water buffaloes help farmers in Shang times?**

WHAT WERE SHANG CITIES LIKE?

Very little remains of ancient Shang buildings and settlements above the ground. Archaeologists have had to dig deeper and it is under the ground where they have found evidence of Shang **architecture**.

The first Shang king, Tang, is thought to have built the city of Shang, near modern-day Zhengzhou. As a symbol of power, this fortified city had walls averaging 10 metres (33 feet) in height, and 20 metres (66 feet) in width. These great walls were made from layers of pounded earth. A thick layer of soil was first put underneath heavy wooden boards, then pounded down to make it compact. The boards were removed and another layer of earth added. Little by little, the city walls grew upwards. It has been calculated that such fortifications would need 10,000 labourers to work for 18 years.

Pan Geng, the nineteenth king of the Shang dynasty, moved his capital to Yin (at modern-day Anyang) in around 1300 BCE. The following eleven Shang kings stayed for more than 250 years at Yin, which is the largest Shang settlement ever built. Eventually, Yin was deserted and the city fell into ruin. Yin is also known as Yin Xu, which means 'ruins of Yin'. Excavations of this ancient Shang city began in 1928.

DETECTIVE WORK

Yin Xu is World Heritage Site number 1114. Find out more at whc. unesco.org/

🐾 **What different materials were used to build roofs in the Shang and Han dynasties?**

This model pottery palace dates from the Han dynasty (from the second century BCE). It shows tiled roofs, but the roofs of Shang houses were thatched.

Early Shang capital cities were divided into separate sections and surrounded by great earth walls. The capital of Yin, from the late Shang period, is quite different. It is protected on one side by the Yellow River, but there is no surrounding city wall. At Yin, smaller buildings form rings around the central palaces and the shrines for royal ancestors.

Unlike the great stone public buildings of ancient Egyptian, Greek or Roman civilizations, these Shang temples and palaces were made out of wood and clay. Frames of timber buildings sat on wooden posts that were rammed into the pounded-earth foundations. Thatched roofs made from tough grasses topped the clay walls. The main halls were at the front of the palaces, with bedrooms to the rear, shrines on the left, and altars to the right.

In 1999, the remains of another Shang city was found at Huanbei, on the other side of the Yellow River. Like the city of Yin, it had pounded-earth foundations, as well as a massive 170-metre-long courtyard area.

Beijing's Forbidden City, built in the fifteenth century CE, shows that the basic shape of Chinese buildings remained unchanged for centuries.

Although the city of Yin was once the greatest Shang capital, it was deserted after the downfall of the Shang dynasty. Ancient Chinese historian Sima Qian explained the reaction of a Chinese king to the ruined city in *Records of the Historian*:

'Seeing the damaged palaces [of Yin Xu] on his way to seek an audience with the king of the Zhou Dynasty, Qi Zi, the king of the Song State wrote a poem titled "Maxi" to express his feelings.'

WHAT WERE 'DRAGON BONES'?

Towards the end of the nineteenth century CE, people found animal bones in fields in Hsiao-t'un, near modern-day Anyang. They were sold as 'dragon bones' and chemists used them to prepare a special medicine. Sometimes these bone fragments had signs scratched on to their surface, so farmers selling the bones to chemists often tried to remove them. Surely 'dragon bones' would not have written marks on them?

DETECTIVE WORK

Discover much more about ancient Chinese oracle bones at http://china.mrdonn.org/oraclebones.html

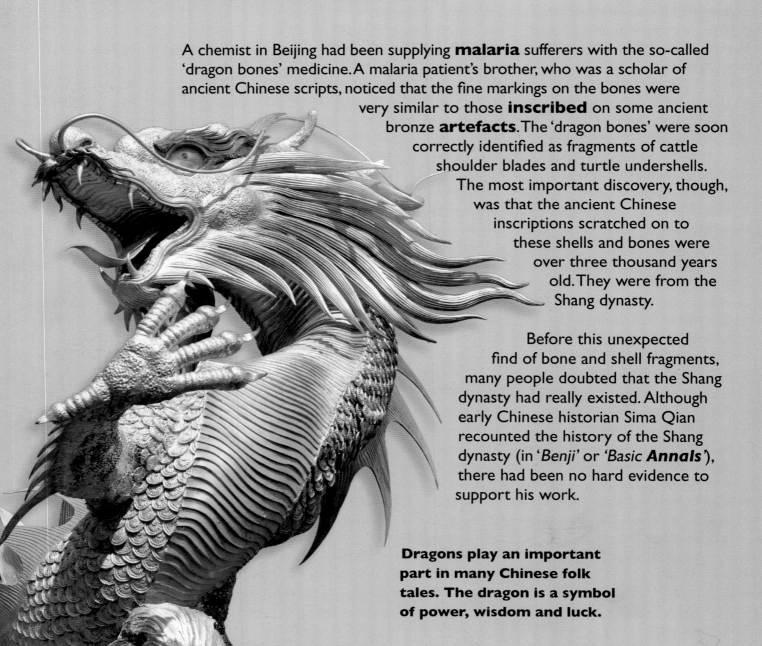

A chemist in Beijing had been supplying **malaria** sufferers with the so-called 'dragon bones' medicine. A malaria patient's brother, who was a scholar of ancient Chinese scripts, noticed that the fine markings on the bones were very similar to those **inscribed** on some ancient bronze **artefacts**. The 'dragon bones' were soon correctly identified as fragments of cattle shoulder blades and turtle undershells. The most important discovery, though, was that the ancient Chinese inscriptions scratched on to these shells and bones were over three thousand years old. They were from the Shang dynasty.

Before this unexpected find of bone and shell fragments, many people doubted that the Shang dynasty had really existed. Although early Chinese historian Sima Qian recounted the history of the Shang dynasty (in '*Benji*' or '*Basic **Annals**'*), there had been no hard evidence to support his work.

Dragons play an important part in many Chinese folk tales. The dragon is a symbol of power, wisdom and luck.

Excavations that took place over many years during the twentieth century unearthed about 100,000 bone and shell fragments. Bit by bit, these fragments – about 7,000 shoulder blades and turtle shells in total – told the history of the ancient dynasty. Although there was little information about ordinary peasants, the bone fragments described royal rituals and ceremonies. They showed the kings' everyday hopes and fears, giving an intriguing insight into the world of the Shang.

Ox shoulder blades and turtle shells were used as part of a ritual. This was carried out to get answers to questions the king might want to ask his ancestor gods. He might want to know, for example, when it was going to rain during a period of drought. He would consult the bones and shells, which are now known as **oracle** bones. A special person called a **diviner** would interpret their replies, or pass the bones to the king so he could decide what the answer was.

You cannot buy 'dragon bones' medicine today. But traditional medicine still plays an important role in Chinese healthcare.

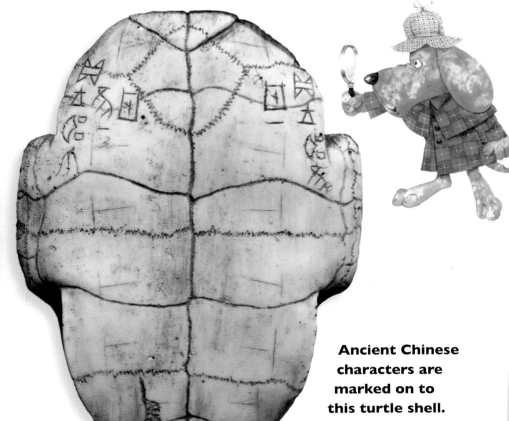

Ancient Chinese characters are marked on to this turtle shell.

Can you see the symbol in the top left repeated anywhere else on the turtle shell?

The discovery of the oracle bones confirmed the existence of the Shang dynasty. In his study on the ancient writings, Chinese scholar Sun I-Jang explained the importance of the find to Chinese history:

'I never dreamed that in my old age I should see such treasure!'

WHAT DID THE BONES SHOW?

Before the discovery of the oracle bones, Shang history was buried and practically unknown. Excited historians started to piece together a picture of royal life in the Shang dynasty. They had also uncovered the earliest known examples of Chinese writings. Many bones had scratched inscriptions of complete sentences in an ancient Chinese script.

Paper was not invented until the second century BCE, when it was created by the Chinese during the Han dynasty. Earlier scripts may have existed on materials like bamboo, wood and silk but none of these remain from Shang times. It is fortunate for historians that the Shang used tougher materials to record the written word. Although some large bronze vessels had inscriptions, most Shang writing was found cut into the oracle bones.

This ancient Chinese writing system used pictographs, or pictures and symbols that stand for a word or thing. A few Chinese symbols inscribed onto the Shang oracle bones were even the same as modern-day Chinese characters. There was now no doubt that ancient Chinese people from the Shang dynasty were using a language that had a direct link to the modern Chinese language.

The Shang writing on this shoulder blade is read in columns from top to bottom.

It is interesting to note how certain Chinese characters have changed a little over time. For example, the Shang character for 'tree' is:

The modern-day Chinese character for 'tree' is:

The symbols are similar, but whereas the modern-day Chinese character shows the tree's roots, the Shang character represents both the roots and branches of the tree.

DETECTIVE WORK

Find out more about ancient Chinese scripts at www.ancientscripts.com/ chinese.html
See how characters for words such as 'rain' and 'moon' were written. Then see how they have developed into modern Chinese script.

Compared to today's more ornate Chinese **calligraphy**, the strokes for each character were also written in a simpler way in Shang times. Many pictographic characters exist in the ancient Shang writing system. There are also characters for ideas, and those made from more than one symbol. Writing from this period is known as Shang modern script. Some Shang writing reads from left to right. Most text inscriptions on oracle bones were written in columns, though, and were meant to be read from top to bottom.

This turtle shell image has a symbol that looks like a stretched-out 'D'. It means 'moon'.

What are the animals at the bottom of the turtle shell?

WHO WERE THE SHANG GODS?

The Shang worshipped their ancestors, who could either protect or punish them. They also praised the gods of nature, including gods of the sun, rain and the Yellow River, or Huang He. But above all the other gods, there was one god called Shang Di, meaning 'Lord on high'.

Shang Di was the supreme god who could cause victory or defeat in battle and the success or failure of harvests. He also controlled the weather, as well as the future of the Shang capital. Not even the Shang kings could contact Shang Di directly. He was far too important. However, Shang Di consulted the royal ancestors of the king, and the king could contact the spirits of his dead family. So in this indirect way, the king discovered the will of the all-powerful god, Shang Di.

During the Shang dynasty, people known as diviners had an important role in helping the king and the royal family. They tried to predict the future for the Shang kings. Diviners used turtle shells and shoulder blades of oxen to carry out divination. The diviner would first cut rows of pits or small hollows on the underside of the bone or shell. He would place the point of a heated rod into certain holes until the bone cracked. The diviner would then be able to interpret the cracks that appeared on the other side of the bone. To the diviner, these random cracks were the answers to certain questions that the king had asked. Following a set question, the diviner's answer could be yes or no, or that something was unknown.

🐾 **What are the small pits in the turtle shell for?**

Shoulder blades and turtle shells were suitable for writing on because they had flat surfaces.

The diviner often cut the words of the question into the bone or shell itself. Sometimes the answer was written, and occasionally the bone was inscribed with both the question and answer. Some diviners would also add a comment on what the actual outcome was. King Wu Ding ruled the Shang kingdom around 1200 BCE and he consulted his royal ancestors through the diviners many times. He asked questions about rainfall, harvests, rituals, curses, dreams, military expeditions and even a royal toothache.

King Wu Ding often consulted the oracle bones. In his book *Ancient China*, historian John Hay gives an example of the sort of questions the king asked:

Divine on the day wu-wu. Ku divined. We are going to hunt at Ch'iu. Any capture?'

There was no answer given on the bones, but the positive outcome of the hunt was recorded:

'The hunt on this day actually captured one tiger, 40 deer, 164 foxes, 159 hornless deer…'

The Shang consulted their gods regularly to see if the weather would help their crops grow.

DETECTIVE WORK

The diviner's job was very important to the king. Discover how the diviner used the oracle bones to help the king divine future events at www.ancientchina.co.uk/writing/explore/oraclebone.html

The Shang worshipped the gods of nature including one for the great Yellow River.

DID THE SHANG SACRIFICE PEOPLE?

The Shang carried out all sorts of ceremonies. They believed that such rituals would bring them rainfall, plentiful harvests, success in battle, or even children and good luck. As they could not worship their all-powerful god Shang Di directly, the members of the royal family honoured their ancestors in frequent ceremonies. These rituals revolved around sacrifices.

The Shang people sacrificed grain, beer and animals – but also people. In around 1200 BCE, when one of their kings died, the Shang prepared an immense tomb to demonstrate the power of their royal ruler. Tomb number 1001 at Anyang needed thousands of labourers to work on it. They dug a cross-shaped pit into the soil more than 90 metres (295 feet) long and up to almost 20 metres (66 feet) deep. Once the enormous pit was ready, the sacrifices could begin. This tomb alone held the remains of 90 followers of the king, who were either buried in coffins or given precious ornaments. A further 74 people, 12 horses and 11 dogs were sacrificed.

DETECTIVE WORK

Find out more about tomb 1001 at Anyang at http://education.asianart. org/explore-resources/ background-information/ tomb-no-1001-anyang You can also take a quick 3D virtual reality tour at www.youtube.com/ watch?v=BOxf4IUiTPo

🐾 **What's inside the bronze pot?**

The Shang are believed to have sacrificed at least 13,000 people during the last 250 years of their dynasty. Bronzes were also an important part of Shang sacrificial rituals.

This pit of oracle bones was discovered at Yin Xu. You can see a human skeleton.

Most oracle bones and the great discoveries around Anyang came to light only in the twentieth century. More than two thousand years ago, the great Chinese thinker Confucius (551 BCE-479 BCE) showed his doubts about Shang culture:

'How can we talk about their ritual? There is a lack of both documents and learned men!'

The **brutality** of the Shang civilization was shown in the way that people were killed as sacrificial victims. On one occasion, the Shang slaughtered 300 slaves from the Qiang tribe in a bloody ritual. In the Hsaio-t'un region, hundreds of human skeletons were discovered among the tombs. Some people had been cut in half, others had been badly **mutilated**. Many had been decapitated, so only headless skeletons remained.

Shang people probably believed that their ancestors enjoyed the bloodshed in these rituals. Those taking part would offer sacrificial food and wine, which was poured into the tomb from bronze wine goblets. The Shang believed that wine, beer, food and blood would revitalize the living and the dead, as the former king passed over into the afterlife. They also thought that the material wealth of the tomb, as well as the many human and animal sacrifices, would lead to a good afterlife for the dead ruler.

This large bronze ritual wine cup is known as a 'gu'. It was used in sacrifices.

WHO WAS LADY FU HAO?

Lady Fu Hao was a brave warrior, a politician and one of King Wu Ding's many wives. She is the first female military leader we know about from historical evidence. One oracle bone inscription tells how she led 13,000 troops into battle against the Qiang.

Fu Hao was also allowed to perform ritual ceremonies. This was unusual for a woman, because this vital part of royal life was usually carried out by men. The king trusted Fu Hao, both as a general and as a priest. But he also respected and loved her as his wife. Oracle bones show the king's concern for her well-being, as he made divinations about her pregnancies and illnesses.

However extraordinary she was when she was alive, Lady Fu Hao has become even more important after her death. Her pit tomb was quite small compared to other royal Shang tombs. It measured about 6 metres (20 feet) by 4 metres (13 feet) at the entrance, and was 8 metres (26 feet) deep. Even so, Lady Fu Hao was buried with many treasures. Other royal tombs have been plundered, but Fu Hao's tomb at Anyang was left intact.

DETECTIVE WORK

Discover more about Fu Hao's tomb's amazing treasures at http://depts.washington.edu/chinaciv/archae/2fuhmain.htm

Many people had to accompany their superiors to the grave while still alive. Recorded in *The Birth of China* by H.G. Creel, an expert on early Chinese civilization, this Chinese poem described an adviser's fear as he had to face his own death in the tomb:

'Who followed Mu to the
     grave?
Tzu-che Chen-hu.
And this Tzu-che Chen-hu
Could withstand a
     hundred men. But when
     he came to the grave,
He looked terrified and
     trembled.'

This is the tomb room at Yin Xu for the great female warrior Lady Fu Hao. The skeletons indicate that many advisers were buried alive with her.

In 1976, archaeologists began to unearth the tomb's magnificent treasures. There were almost 2,000 items buried with Fu Hao. The most valuable artefacts were over 460 bronze objects including more than 130 battle weapons, 27 knives and 23 bells. There were more than 750 carved jade ornaments and jewellery, over 500 bone carvings including hairpins and arrowheads, as well as ivory objects, pottery and almost 7,000 cowry shells.

Within the tomb chamber, the corpse of Lady Fu Hao was set in a coffin, which has since decayed. A pit below the corpse held the skeletons of six dogs. 16 humans, buried alive, also died in the tomb. It was thought that such sacrifices and treasures would help to ensure a happy afterlife for Lady Fu Hao.

The 'HouMuWu' is a massive square vessel, or 'ding' ('Mu' is another name for Fu Hao). Found in the tomb, this bronze weighs 875 kg (1,929 lb).

This bronze ritual wine container from Fu Hao's tomb is shaped like an owl.

🐾 **What do you think the two figures that face each other are on the vessel's handles? There is a human head between their jaws, in the middle, at the top.**

WHAT ART DID THE SHANG MAKE?

The Shang produced good-quality pottery, including white-glazed bowls and dishes for their rituals. They also made a tougher grey pottery for everyday use. Jade carving became quite advanced too. Skilled craftspeople also produced a wide range of bronze items, including bells and axes, but by far the most impressive were the large bronze vessels for food and wine.

Shang artisans carved the green stone jade into many beautiful objects. They made some of the oldest examples, producing ceremonial weapons or delicately shaped handles for daggers. The ancient Chinese believed that jade ornaments helped the dead to have a long and happy existence in the afterlife. There are many animal carvings including tigers, rhinoceroses, water buffaloes and elephants, as well as human figures. The Shang also carved wooden, bone and ivory pieces. Some examples are decorated with blue-coloured stones called turquoise. They also created larger marble sculptures with animal designs.

Some vases were made from the ivory of elephant tusks.

What are the blue stones in the vase called?

Jade was prized by the Shang for its beauty. Craftspeople usually carved it into animal shapes.

DETECTIVE WORK

Whether they were carving jade or casting bronze, Shang craftspeople were very gifted. Discover more by viewing a slideshow of some examples of their work at www.metmuseum.org/ toah/hd/shzh/hd_shzh. htm#slideshow1

The most spectacular bronzes of this period would not have existed without the art of pottery. The Shang made many large bronze vessels that had to be cast, or shaped, by pouring the **molten** metal into a mould. First they made a pottery model and a decorated mould to go on the outside, leaving a narrow gap for the melted bronze to fill. The Shang artist would have carved his own unique patterns, forms and decorations on the pottery mould. These would then transfer on to the outer surface of the bronze vessel. This was a very tricky technique in itself, but the artist would first need to cast the bronze's legs and handles before casting the main body of the bowl on to them.

Shang bronzes often included animal masks in their designs. Although some pieces are similar, each was individually created. The great range of bronze pieces discovered shows that Shang craftspeople were not simply skilled technicians. They were artists of incredible quality.

Many of the bronze vessels made during the late Shang period had an inscription, such as this simple one for an ancestor:

'A vessel made for Father Hsin.'

This large, ornate bronze vessel can be seen at Shanghai Museum in China.

WHAT'S SO SPECIAL ABOUT SHANG BRONZE-WORK?

The Shang's brilliance in making these bronzes sets this civilization apart from earlier times, when people used simple stone and flint tools. The level of skill of the bronze-work shows us how advanced Chinese culture was during the Shang dynasty. It explains why this period is known as China's Bronze Age.

Bronze was highly valued, rare and was quite difficult to produce in this area of ancient China. An **alloy** of metals, bronze is a mixture of copper, tin and a little lead. Shang kings and nobles organized large numbers of men to mine the metal **ores** with basic digging tools. The ores were then transported from the different places to furnaces where they were heated, refined and combined in the correct quantities to produce bronze.

The Shang craftspeople made ornate bronze weapons, cups, vases and musical instruments, such as bells and drums. They also created many large bronze ritual vessels reserved for special rituals and ceremonies. Despite the technical difficulty in making these huge bronze vessels, the finished product was often perfect. Decorations range from straight horizontal lines to **geometric** patterns and intricate raised surfaces. The designs are almost always **symmetrical**.

This ornate ceremonial axe-head may have been used as a weapon of execution.

DETECTIVE WORK

The large bronze vessels were perhaps the greatest achievement of the Shang dynasty. By the late Shang period, what sort of things did the rulers inscribe on these vessels? Research more about bronzes at www.chinaonlinemuseum.com/bronzes-shang.php

The main design element of a bronze is the animal mask. There are many examples of all types of animals, including rams, water buffaloes and tigers, as well as some monstrous-looking heads. Unlike earlier images of animal heads seen from the side, the creature is shown from the front. They are the earliest known examples of this type of design.

Bronzes made during the early Shang period are the most simplified. It is astonishing, though, to see how quickly ancient Chinese craftspeople developed their skills in bronze-work. The magnificent Bronze Age treasures found in the tombs in modern-day Anyang (originally Yin) date from the late Shang era, around the eleventh century BCE. Here the animal masks are no longer simplified, but have intricate patterns. Some bronzes bear inscriptions, with the same writing as the oracle bones. Along with the oracle bones, the Shang dynasty's bronzes are the most remarkable of ancient Shang treasures.

This bronze wine container shows different animal shapes, including a dragon.

This is a 'li', which means a three-legged pot. It is based on a pottery cooking vessel, unique to north China.

Bronze artefacts discovered in this region of China are exceptional. Chinese art historian and archaeologist Robert Bagley describes the unique nature of the finds from the Shang era:

"Nothing remotely comparable is known elsewhere in the ancient world."

🐾 **Is the design of this bronze pot irregular or symmetrical?**

YOUR PROJECT

By now you may have already collected lots of information about the Shang dynasty and life in ancient China. What sort of project would you like to do on this fascinating topic?

You might decide to create your own project on Yin Xu, or perhaps the recent discovery at nearby Huanbei. Find out more about Lady Fu Hao's amazing tomb discoveries, or imagine you are a loyal follower of Lady Fu Hao. She has just died and you too will have to follow her to the tomb. What are your feelings? What can you see in the tomb? Are there any more people or any live animals entombed with you?

Alternatively, find a particular piece of Shang craftsmanship, such as a bronze. Decide what you like about it. Concentrate on it. Try drawing or making a model of it. Do some research on the Internet. When and where was the item found? Was it uncovered in a pit tomb? What was it used for? Were there any other treasures found nearby?

Or, you may prefer to find out more about Chinese pictographs and calligraphy. Alternatively, imagine you are an expert in Chinese writing. You are the person to make the discovery that strange 'dragon bones' have an ancient form of Chinese writing inscribed on them.

Still undecided about what to do? Remember, whatever you decide, this is your project. So pick an area that really interests you.

This bronze axe-head with ornate decorations dates from the late Shang era.

Project presentation

● Do lots of research before you begin your project. Use the Internet, as well as your local and school library.

● Find out about Huanbei. You might want to start with the news article at: www.independent.co.uk/life-style/history/human-sacrifices-discovered-at-torched-shang-dynasty-city-huanbei-1975492.html
You can do further research about Huanbei as a World Heritage Site at: whc.unesco.org/

● If you decide to look at calligraphy, try to research some ancient Chinese symbols. Do some of these look like simplified pictures of the word? Can you see how a modern Chinese word is related to an ancient character?

● Whatever your project, compile a list of useful websites and other sources of information.

Research online about the National Museum of Chinese Writing, in Anyang, China.

The British Museum in London has many Chinese artefacts, including some from the Shang era.

GLOSSARY

alloy A mixture of metals.

ambitious Really wanting to succeed.

ancestors Forefathers, or members of a family that have lived at an earlier time.

annals Yearly records, or history, of events.

archaeologists People who study the remains of past societies.

architecture Buildings.

artefacts Things made by people, such as a tool or work of art.

BCE 'Before the Common Era'. Used to signify years before the believed birth of Jesus, around 2,000 years ago.

Bronze Age The period when people learned to work metal. In China, this was around the time of the Shang dynasty.

brutality Vicious behaviour.

calligraphy Handwriting.

CE 'Common Era'. Used to signify years since the believed birth of Jesus.

clan A group of people who are related.

culture Beliefs, arts and ways of living of a particular group.

depraved Corrupt.

discernment Keen judgement.

disposition Someone's usual state of mind.

dissolute Poor or wayward behaviour.

diviner Someone who predicts the future.

excavations Digs.

exploited Used, or taken advantage of.

geometric Using simple forms such as circles and rectangles.

infantry Foot soldiers.

inscribed Carved or engraved.

inscription Engraved writing.

livestock Kept animals, such as cattle and horses.

malaria A disease caused by mosquito bites.

molten Melted.

mutilated Damaged, cut up.

oracle Prophecy or answer from god.

ores Rocks from which metal can be extracted.

rituals Ceremonies.

sacrifices Ritual or ceremonial killings.

symmetrical Showing symmetry, or the ability to reflect an image exactly about a point or a line.

vessels Pots generally used to hold liquids.

ANSWERS

Page 5:   Yellow River. It is named after the large amount of yellow silt deposited around the river's mouth.
Page 7:   Horses.
Page 8:   Bronze.
Page 11:   It is thought that Shang farmers may have used water buffaloes and oxen to help them farm the land. The animals probably pulled an early plough.
Page 12:   Han roofs were covered with tiles. Shang buildings would have had thatched roofs made from grasses.
Page 15:   It is repeated in the top right. The symbol means 'divine' – the script below shows what subject is being divined on this oracle bone.
Page 17:   Birds.
Page 18:   The diviner would place a hot poker into one of the pits when divining. He would then read the cracks that developed in the shell.
Page 20:   Broken pieces of a human skull.
Page 23:   They are meant to be two tigers.
Page 24:   Turquoise – the same name as the colour.
Page 27:   Symmetrical.

FURTHER INFORMATION

Books to read
Ancient China (The Ancient World) by Liz Sonneborn (Scholastic, 2012)
Ancient China (Hands-on Ancient History) by James Anderson (Heinemann Library, 2007)
Ancient China (True Books: Ancient Civilizations) by Mel Friedman (Scholastic, 2010)
Ancient China (DK Eyewitness Books) by Arthur Cotterell (Dorling Kindersley, 2005)

Websites
www.education.com/study-help/article/ancient-history-china-shang-dynasty/
www.slideshare.net/Gregman215/shang-dynasty-presentation
http://totallyhistory.com/shang-dynasty-1556-1046-bc/
Note to parents and teachers: Every effort has been made by the publishers to ensure that these websites are suitable for children. However, because of the nature of the Internet, it is impossible to guarantee that the contents of these sites will not be altered. We strongly advise that Internet access is supervised by a responsible adult.

Places to visit
British Museum, London, WC1B 3DG
Yin Xu, Henan Province, China

INDEX

Numbers in **bold** refer to pictures and captions

THE HISTORY DETECTIVE INVESTIGATES

Contents of all the titles in the series: